ENHANCING WOMEN-FOCUSED INVESTMENTS IN CLIMATE AND DISASTER RESILIENCE

MAY 2020

Canada

ADB

© 2020 Asian Development Bank
6 ADB Avenue, Mandaluyong City, 1550 Metro Manila, Philippines
Tel +63 2 8632 4444; Fax +63 2 8636 2444
www.adb.org

Some rights reserved. Published in 2020.

ISBN 978-92-9262-211-4 (print); 978-92-9262-212-1 (electronic); 978-92-9262-213-8 (ebook)
Publication Stock No. TCS200140-2
DOI: http://dx.doi.org/10.22617/TCS200140-2

The views expressed in this publication are those of the authors and do not necessarily reflect the views and policies of the Asian Development Bank (ADB) or its Board of Governors or the governments they represent.

ADB does not guarantee the accuracy of the data included in this publication and accepts no responsibility for any consequence of their use. The mention of specific companies or products of manufacturers does not imply that they are endorsed or recommended by ADB in preference to others of a similar nature that are not mentioned.

By making any designation of or reference to a particular territory or geographic area, or by using the term "country" in this document, ADB does not intend to make any judgments as to the legal or other status of any territory or area.

Please contact pubsmarketing@adb.org if you have questions or comments with respect to content, or if you wish to obtain copyright permission for your intended use that does not fall within these terms, or for permission to use the ADB logo.

Corrigenda to ADB publications may be found at http://www.adb.org/publications/corrigenda.

Notes:
In this publication, "$" refers to US dollars.
All photos are from the Asian Development Bank

Cover design by Lowil Espada. On the cover: Doan Thi Out, harvesting unit team leader, at the Dalat Hasfarm in Lam Dong, Viet Nam. The High-Value Horticulture Development Project will introduce and transfer a successful high-value horticulture business model built on the introduction of climate-resilient greenhouse technology.

Contents

Tables, Figures, and Box

Tables

Figures

Box

Foreword

Women play important roles for leading actions to strengthen resilience to disaster and climate-related shocks and stresses, especially at the local level. Such actions create transformational change by challenging existing standards and paradigms and concur with the objectives of the Sustainable Development Goals, the Paris Agreement, and the Sendai Framework for Disaster Risk Reduction. However, investments in such actions remain limited.

This report focuses on women as agents of change for resilient development, and argues for more investments in enhancing their capacities. Women-focused investments in climate and disaster resilience require tackling multiple vulnerabilities and discriminations that women and girls face in the near and longer term. Such investments should be undertaken in all sectors—agriculture and livelihoods, urban, energy, water resources, finance, and social protection—and require political will, technical capacity, wide-ranging partnerships, and longer-term commitment.

Investing in women-focused resilience-building measures is not a choice, but rather an imperative for increasing resilience outcomes and advancing sustainable development.

Under Strategy 2030, the Asian Development Bank is set to increase the number of operations addressing climate change challenges and promoting gender equality. Each of these areas of operations need to reach at least 75% of overall committed operations by 2030. To achieve these twin targets, women-focused climate and disaster resilience building is essential.

We hope the report contributes to useful debates on how women-focused resilience building can be expanded in Asia and the Pacific.

Preety M. Bhandari
Chief of Climate Change and Disaster Risk
Management Thematic Group
Asian Development Bank

Sonomi Tanaka
Chief of Gender Development Thematic Group
Asian Development Bank

Acknowledgments

This report is based on the experiences of the Integrated Disaster Risk Management Fund, which is financed by the Government of Canada and administered by the Asian Development Bank (ADB).

The report was prepared under the overall guidance of Arghya Sinha Roy, senior climate change specialist (climate change adaptation), Sustainable Development and Climate Change Department (SDCC), ADB; and Zonibel Woods, consultant and senior social development specialist (gender and development), (SDCC). Special thanks to Chandy Chea, senior social development officer (Gender), Southeast Asia Department (SERD) and Riana Puspasari, gender consultant (SERD) for their support and inputs in developing the report.

Yue Cao (consultant) and Emma Lovell (consultant) from the Overseas Development Institute (ODI) developed the draft of the report, based on inputs received from various stakeholders. The manuscript was edited by Karen Williams. The infographic and layout were done by Lowil Espada.

The report benefited significantly from comments by Carmen Leon-Himmelstine, ODI, Mairi MacCrae, social development specialist (gender), Pacific Regional Department (PARD) and Joanne Quintana, gender consultant, South East Asia Regional Department, ADB. Thanks also to Laurence Levague, senior social development specialist (gender and development), Southeast Asia Department, ADB, for her initial contributions to this initiative. Special thanks to the contributions of the participants in a regional workshop in Bangkok (January 2019) that included government representatives from Cambodia, Indonesia, Myanmar, the Lao People's Democratic Republic, the Philippines, and Viet Nam, as well as experts from various development organizations.

Abbreviations

ADB	Asian Development Bank
CCA	climate change adaptation
CSA	climate-smart agriculture
DMC	developing member country
DRM	disaster risk management
FAO	Food and Agriculture Organization of the United Nations
GDP	gross domestic product
NGO	nongovernment organization
O&M	operation and maintenance
SDG	Sustainable Development Goal

1 | INTRODUCTION

Women fetch water during a very dry season in Myanmar.

1.1 Why This Report?

As climate and disaster risks increase, they affect the lives and livelihoods of millions of people, especially the marginalized. For various interrelating factors, women are more vulnerable to the impact of disasters and climate change. Women are often poorer than their male counterparts and have lower levels of economic participation. In Asia, women account for two thirds of the poor and 80% of all people living on under $2 per day (UN Women 2018). Women's economic activity is highly concentrated in agriculture, the sector highly vulnerable to the impacts of disasters and climate change. On the other hand, evidence shows that women lead resilience strategies that deal with disaster- and climate-related shocks and stresses, especially at the local level. In many cases, women exhibit leadership as beneficiaries of government's pro-poor development programs; and as active members of community-based organizations working closely with local governments, civil society organizations, and the private sector to address adaptation efforts.

Investing more, and in a targeted manner, in women can help increase resilience. Given women's social roles, they are challenged by and have a deeper understanding of rural and urban vulnerabilities. This is the starting point of any resilience investment. Understanding the nature of gender-based vulnerabilities is crucial to recognizing the diverse impact of climate change and disasters on the population. Gender-based vulnerabilities are not natural and intrinsic, but rather stem from sociocultural discrimination and inequitable practices. Women are more dependent on natural ecosystems for their livelihoods and, hence, have a better understanding of the functions they provide, including regulatory functions to deal with shocks and stresses. Resilience interventions (structural and nonstructural) prioritized by women do not focus exclusively on women's issues but on family and community issues, thereby advancing wider development. In other words, women-led resilience-building strategies bundle solutions to manage multiple vulnerabilities in the near and longer term for women and communities.

This report focuses on women as agents of change for resilient development and argues for more investments in their existing capacities. This concurs with the global development agenda of the Sustainable Development Goals (SDGs), the Paris Agreement on Climate Change, and the Sendai Framework for Disaster Risk Reduction. However, substantial gaps remain in the ability of many countries and communities to generate the necessary political will; technical capacity; and commitment to design, finance, and implement gender-responsive policies and programs to tackle climate change and increase resilience to disasters (ADB and Huairou Commission 2017).

If women-focused investments in climate and disaster resilience are to be truly transformative, they must address harmful gender norms at the root of women's individual and structural vulnerabilities (ADB and UN Women 2018; Bradshaw and Fordham 2013; Le Masson et al. 2016). Climate and disaster resilience represent an opportunity to promote positive change toward gender equality and challenge historical patriarchal norms and practices. These goals could be achieved by shifting consideration of the role of women affected by disaster from "vulnerable" and "victim" to "game changer" and "active stakeholder."

This report aims to (i) reinforce the dialogue on the importance of women-focused investments in climate and disaster resilience, (ii) identify key characteristics of such investments, and (iii) discuss the wider enabling environment that can make such investments effective.

1.2 Who Is This Report For?

The report primarily aims to inform senior officials from sector ministries and their counterparts in ministries of planning and finance in Southeast Asian developing member countries (DMCs) of the Asian Development Bank (ADB). Most sectors (i.e., agriculture; rural development, social protection, urban development, forestry, and water resources management) provide opportunities to strengthen women's resilience. Such opportunities should be realized through public and private investments that combine structural and nonstructural interventions.

The report targets senior officials from national agencies responsible for gender and development, climate change adaptation (CCA), and disaster risk management (DRM). While these ministries and/or agencies typically are not responsible for undertaking investment projects, it is important that officials (i) understand the importance of such investments; (ii) advocate for such investments with their colleagues from different sector ministries and ministries of planning and finance; and (iii) support sector ministries in development and implementation of investment projects through relevant data, information, and learnings. Enhancing officials' understanding is critical for ensuring prioritization of women-related resilience considerations in relevant policy, legislation, and plans for gender and development, climate change, and DRM.

This report also targets ADB sector specialists working in Southeast Asian countries to support the development and implementation of investment projects. Working closely with gender, climate change, and DRM specialists, sector specialists can generate evidence, understand benefits, identify opportunities, and create impetus for women-focused investments in resilience. Development partners, including global funds that support gender and resilient development, may find this report useful.

1.3 What Approach Was Adopted to Develop This Report?

This report is based on a review of existing literature on (i) the nexus of climate and disaster risk, poverty, and gender equality; (ii) a review of gender, climate, and disaster resilience policy and regulations in the context of two Southeast Asian developing countries, Cambodia and Indonesia; and (iii) key-informant interviews with government stakeholders and development partners in the same countries.

The review guided analysis of the type of features women-focused investments in climate and disaster resilience should possess and how, in concrete terms, these investments can be delivered through different sectors under the leadership of government line ministries. The analysis was presented, corroborated, and refined during discussions at a regional workshop on Strengthening Women-Focused Investments in Climate and Disaster Resilience[1] (January 2019, Bangkok) and attended by government officials from six DMCs,[2] including those from ministries and/or national agencies of planning and finance, agriculture and rural development, urban development, women and development, DRM, and CCA, as well as by development partners.

---

1   Organized by ADB in partnership with the Overseas Development Institute, and with financial support from the Government of Canada.
2   Cambodia, Indonesia, the Lao People's Democratic Republic (Lao PDR), Myanmar, the Philippines, and Viet Nam.

1.4   What Common Terms Does This Report Use?

Table 1.   Definition of Common Term

Terms	Definition and Explanation
Climate change	A change of climate, which is attributed directly or indirectly to human activity that alters the composition of the global atmosphere and which is in addition to natural climate variability observed over comparable time periods (United Nations 1992, p.7). For the purposes of this report, "climate change" also encompasses natural climate variability when the latter is not specified in the rest of the report. (Source: United Nations Framework Convention on Climate Change [UNFCCC]).
Climate change adaptation	In human systems, the process of adjusting to actual or expected climate change and its effects to moderate harm or exploit beneficial opportunities. In natural systems, the process of adjustment to actual climate and its effects; human intervention may facilitate adjustment to expected climate (Source: Intergovernmental Panel on Climate Change [IPCC] 2012).
Disaster risk management	The application of disaster risk reduction policies and strategies to prevent new disaster risk, reduce existing disaster risk, and manage residual risk, contributing to the strengthening of resilience and reduction of disaster losses (Source: United Nations Office for Disaster Risk Reduction [UNISDR]).
Resilience	The ability of a system, community, or society to resist, absorb, accommodate, adapt, transform, and recover from the effects of a hazard in a timely and efficient manner, including through the preservation and restoration of its essential basic structures and functions through risk management (Source: UNISDR).
Shocks	Sudden, sharp events that threaten a community. In this document, shocks refer to those triggered by natural hazards (Source: Adapted from 100 Resilient Cities webpage).
Stresses	Factors that weaken the fabric of a community on a daily or cyclical basis. In this document, stresses refer to those that originate in changes in climate variables (Source: Adapted from 100 Resilient Cities webpage).
Vulnerability	The conditions determined by physical, social, economic, and environmental factors or processes that increase the susceptibility of an individual, a community, assets, or systems to the impacts of hazards (Source: UNISDR).

2 | WOMEN-FOCUSED INVESTMENT IN RESILIENCE: WHY DOES IT MATTER?

A villager crosses the river using a makeshift raft in Mingaladon Township, Yangon, Myanmar.

2.1 Climate and Disaster Risks Undermine Efforts to Achieve Sustainable Development

Disasters triggered by natural hazards, including those influenced by natural climate variability and anthropogenic climate change, have significant immediate and long-term impacts that can reverse years of gains in key development sectors. The Southeast Asia region is highly prone to geophysical (e.g., earthquakes, tsunamis, volcanic eruptions) and hydrometeorological (e.g., tropical cyclones, droughts, floods) hazards. Over the last 3 decades, natural hazard-related disasters caused about 403,000 deaths, affected the lives and livelihoods of millions of people, and caused huge economic losses. Importantly, socially constructed gender-specific vulnerabilities have contributed to higher mortality rates for women in disasters (Neumayer and Plümper 2007). On the other hand, climate change and variability exacerbate existing stresses on water resources, agriculture, and coastal management through slow-onset changes in rainfall patterns, temperatures, and rising sea levels (Gass et al. 2011). Further, climate and disaster risks likely will increase in intensity and complexity when combined with other development challenges (e.g., growing inequality, continuing environmental degradation, inadequate social services, infrastructure deficits). Lacking effective management of climate change and disaster risks, their impact will continue to undermine efforts to reduce poverty and achieve sustainable development (ADB and Huairou Commission 2017).

2.2 Women Are Key to Driving Inclusive Resilience Strategies at the Local Level

Addressing climate and disaster risks requires investments that build resilience by (i) targeting the most vulnerable; (ii) tapping local knowledge, capacities, and resources; and (iii) focusing on a combination of structural and nonstructural measures to produce multiple benefits over different time frames. Women play a critical role in advancing such investments, especially at the local level. Women's roles provide invaluable knowledge and capacities to identify and address the underlying drivers of vulnerability in households, communities, and the wider society. Increasing evidence from developing countries in Southeast Asia (e.g., Indonesia, the Philippines, and Viet Nam) suggests that grassroots women's organizations collaborate closely with local governments to use this knowledge and build capacity to assess, prioritize, negotiate, and influence resource allocation for resilience investments targeted at vulnerable communities. These investments do not focus exclusively on women but aim to improve the lives of their families and communities. More importantly, the strategies adopted by women highlight their leadership role in claiming resources and public recognition, thereby shifting the view of women's status from victims and passive beneficiaries to stakeholders and drivers of resilient development. (Huairou Commission and ADB 2017). Other evidence shows the crucial role women play post-disaster as providers, leaders, and managers, and it is important that investments promote these capacities (ADB and UN Women 2018; Bradshaw and Fordham 2013; Chanthy and Samchan 2014; GGCA 2016; Huairou Commission 2015).

Women's resilience to climate change and disasters could be further enhanced through community-based interventions aimed at strengthening livelihoods and communities' adaptive capacity, taking into account social, economic, and environmental features as well as local development priorities. Such interventions may encompass cross-sector and integrated measures such as (i) developing climate change-resilient livelihoods; (ii) policy advocacy to strengthen disaster risk governance; (iii) activities to strengthen women's self-reliance, leadership, and confidence; and (iv) enhancing communities' well-being, health care, and adaptive capacity. In Bangladesh, Oxfam is implementing the second phase of Resilience through Economic Empowerment, Climate Adaptation, Leadership and Learning. This program integrates women's economic empowerment and leadership, climate change adaptation, and disaster risk reduction through diverse interventions (e.g., strengthening economic empowerment through agricultural value-chains, savings, and leadership training; and raising awareness of eco-friendly and climate-adaptive agriculture technology).

2.3 Women-Focused Investments in Resilience Remain Limited

Despite increasing evidence on the crucial role of women in strengthening resilience, investments that focus on women remain limited. Existing national CCA and DRM policies, as well as sector plans and policies, often do not consider women's role in resilience building an explicit priority. There is a strong need for effective programs aimed at increasing women's resilience while addressing their vulnerabilities and boosting their adaptive capacity. Such programs should be (i) informed by collection and analysis of sex-disaggregated data, (ii) implemented using a rights-based approach, and (iii) designed through inclusive processes that engage women at all levels of decision-making.

Evidence shows that further investment in women's capacities is critical not only for managing the risks of climate change and disasters (GGCA 2016), but also for contributing more broadly to national development (Williams 2011). In Bangladesh, a 2017 CCA study found that projects that prioritized gender equality were 37% more effective at increasing women's opportunities to access economic resources and leadership positions, strengthening community capacity, and building resilience to climate impacts than control projects that did not have such objectives (UN Women 2017). From a sector perspective, a study by the Food and Agriculture Organization of the United Nations (FAO 2011) shows that women and men with the same access to productive resources can increase yields on their farms by 20%–30%. This could increase total agricultural output in developing countries by 2.5%–4%, which in turn could reduce the number of hungry people by 12%–17% worldwide (FAO 2011). Globally, investing in women's equality would add $12 trillion (11%) to global gross domestic product (GDP) by 2025 (McKinsey 2015). The regional GDP of Asia and the Pacific would rise $4.5 trillion, a 12% increase over a business-as-usual trajectory (Woetzel et al. 2018).

Thus, to achieve the 2030 Agenda for Sustainable Development, it is essential that developing countries in Southeast Asia promote policies and investments that address "structural issues such as unfair social norms and attitudes as well as developing progressive legal frameworks that promote equality between women and men" (United Nations 2018, p.4) in all areas of life, including resilience to climate change and disasters, to ensure that "no one is left behind" (United Nations 2018, p.6).

2.4 Gender and Resilience Are Cornerstones of ADB Strategy 2030

Accelerating progress in gender equality and building climate and disaster resilience are two of the seven operational priorities of ADB's Strategy 2030. Both priorities have quantitative targets for (i) gender: by 2030, at least 75% of the number of ADB's committed operations (on a 3-year rolling average, including both sovereign and nonsovereign operations) will promote gender equality; and (ii) climate change: 75% of committed operations (on a 3-year rolling average, including sovereign and nonsovereign operations) will support climate change mitigation and adaptation by 2030; and climate finance from ADB's own resources will reach $80 billion cumulatively from 2019 to 2030 (ADB 2018).

3 | WHAT DO WE MEAN BY WOMEN-FOCUSED INVESTMENTS IN RESILIENCE?

Biodiversity Conservation Corridors Initiative Corridors at the Xe Pian–Dong Hua Sao site. Sisouk Southavy grows mushrooms near her home in Xe Pian, Lao People's Democratic Republic.

3.1 Defining Women-Focused Investment in Resilience

This report defines women-focused investments in climate and disaster resilience as investments that explicitly strengthen the resilience of women, particularly poor women, and/or investments that are led by women and advance their resilience to climate change and disasters. Figure 1 shows examples of potential investments in the public and private sectors. These investments include a wide range of interventions that build women's capacities and resilience to disasters and climate change (e.g., human resources, institutional strengthening, financial literacy, promotion of women's voice and representation, skill development, learning). To be fully mainstreamed into the economy and contribute to wider inclusive and socioeconomic development, implementation should be based in a robust understanding of climate and disaster risk and through relevant sectors.

3.2 Women-Focused Investment in Resilience Requires Moving Beyond Gender Mainstreaming

Focusing on women means prioritizing investment projects where the primary stakeholders are women throughout the project cycle—planning, design, implementation, monitoring, evaluation, and learning (for operational guidance, see Box 1). This differs from the conventional approach of gender mainstreaming, where gender actions are considered an "add-on" to investments, with women receiving only "co-benefits" of interventions. However, this does not mean that women-focused investments in climate and disaster resilience should work in isolation from men. While prioritizing women, interventions need to work with men to help challenge discriminatory gender norms and ensure effectiveness and sustainability, while not antagonizing power relations within the household and community (ADB and UN Women 2018). Additionally, interventions should address women's heterogeneity:

Figure 1. Examples of Women-Focused Investments in Resilience

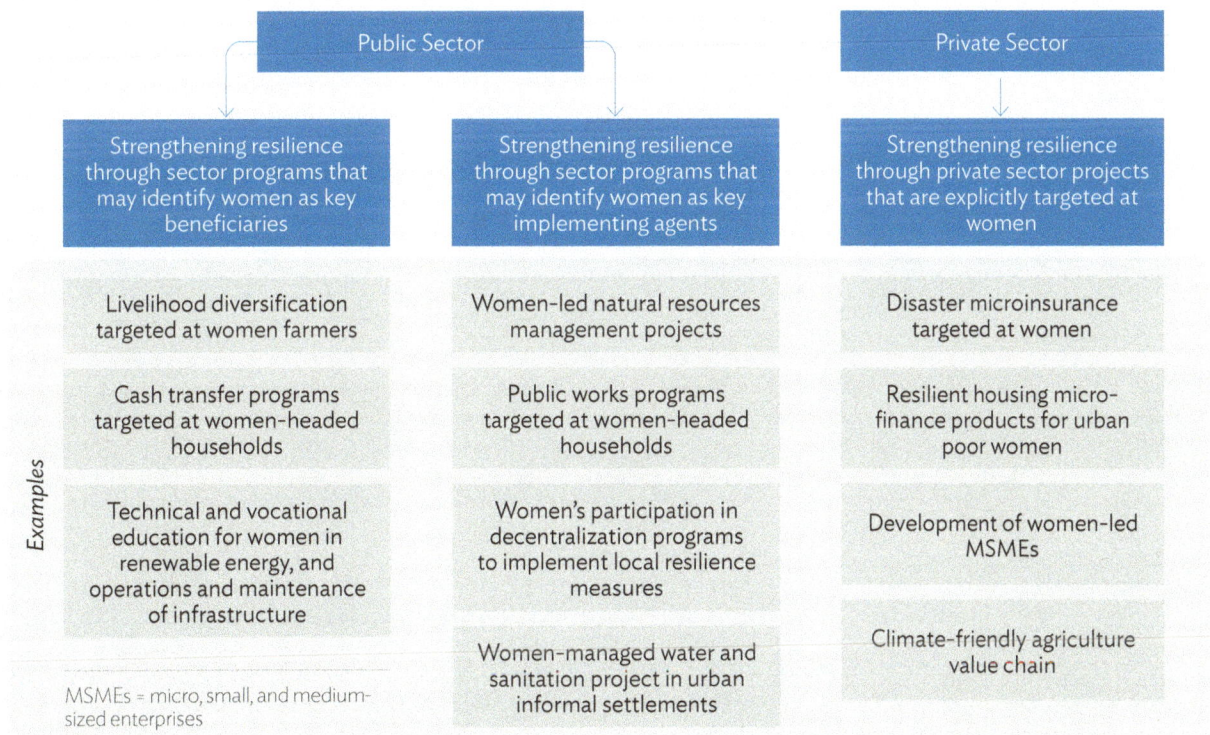

Public Sector

Private Sector

Strengthening resilience through sector programs that may identify women as key beneficiaries

Strengthening resilience through sector programs that may identify women as key implementing agents

Strengthening resilience through private sector projects that are explicitly targeted at women

Examples

Livelihood diversification targeted at women farmers

Women-led natural resources management projects

Disaster microinsurance targeted at women

Cash transfer programs targeted at women-headed households

Public works programs targeted at women-headed households

Resilient housing micro-finance products for urban poor women

Technical and vocational education for women in renewable energy, and operations and maintenance of infrastructure

Women's participation in decentralization programs to implement local resilience measures

Development of women-led MSMEs

Women-managed water and sanitation project in urban informal settlements

Climate-friendly agriculture value chain

MSMEs = micro, small, and medium-sized enterprises

Source: ADB.

9

individuals will have different interests, needs, skills, and capacities, and different access to the range of services and systems that will support their well-being in the face of disaster- and climate-related shocks and stresses (Le Masson 2015). The Gender Action Plan adopted at the 23rd Conference of the Parties to the UNFCCC (6–17 November, 2017, Bonn, Germany) calls for the design and implementation of gender-responsive climate finance strategies, identification of women's needs for support and capacity building, and full inclusion of women in the development of those financial plans.

3.3 Women-Focused Investment in Resilience Aims for Transformational Change

The Intergovernmental Panel on Climate Change (IPCC) Special Report on Global Warming of 1.5°C stresses that limiting the unprecedented risks that temperature rise to date poses to vulnerable people and groups (sometimes including, women) will require "substantial societal and technological transformations" (Allen et al. 2018, p.56). In other words, generating incremental improvements alone is no longer sufficient, and women-focused investments must aim to create transformational change. In this case, transformational change refers to actions and behaviors that challenge existing standards and general paradigms (and disrupt old path dependencies) to increase women's resilience. From a gender perspective, this means moving away from "considering women as victims of climate change and disasters to acknowledging structural inequalities (and their drivers) that impede women's capacities to actively build their resilience along with that of their family and community . . . when projects aim to achieve gender equality and explicitly promote women's empowerment, they tend to recognize the influence of social norms on people's capacities to build resilience. In other words, when activities aim to tackle harmful norms, this translates into a more transformative agenda" (Le Masson 2016, p. 28).

Box 1. Identifying Women-Focused Investment Projects for Strengthening Resilience

The following questions can guide sector specialists from government agencies and development partners as they formulate women-focused investments for strengthening resilience:

- Is your sector impacted by climate change and disaster risks? How is the impact felt by people (e.g., through infrastructure damage, livelihood and income losses, longer-term loss of well-being)? Is there evidence that the impact is disproportionately felt by women in the community? If yes, what are the root causes for such disproportionate impact? Can sector-specific intervention targeted at women help reduce such impact in the future? Can women-centric interventions in other sectors help reduce such impact (which will benefit your sector too)? If yes, which sector/s? Note: Not all impacts are visible in the short run, especially the impact of slow-onset climate changes such as temperature increase and sea-level rise.
- Is your sector impacted by climate change and disaster risk? What type of interventions (structural and nonstructural) in your sector can help manage such risks? How important is it to involve women in such interventions? For example, are women the key labor force in the impacted sector or subsector? How can women's knowledge be tapped in designing the intervention? Can women be engaged in implementing specific aspects of the interventions? Describe the full range of benefits that your intervention can produce if it targeted women as the implementing agent.

The following questions can guide private sector specialists in developing women-focused investments for strengthening resilience:

- Do you see business opportunities in your field for creating products that can strengthen resilience? If yes, do you see women as potential clients of such products? How can the potential products be designed specifically to cater to the needs of women? What type of support might you need from the government and/or development partners to develop such products?
- Are women the primary clients of your business? If yes, are they impacted by climate and disaster risks, which also impacts the performance of your business? What type of support might they need to adapt to the risks? Can you develop products to provide such support as part of and linked to your existing product line? What type of support might you need from the government and/or development partners to develop such products?

Source: ADB.

4 | CHARACTERISTICS OF WOMEN-FOCUSED INVESTMENTS IN RESILIENCE

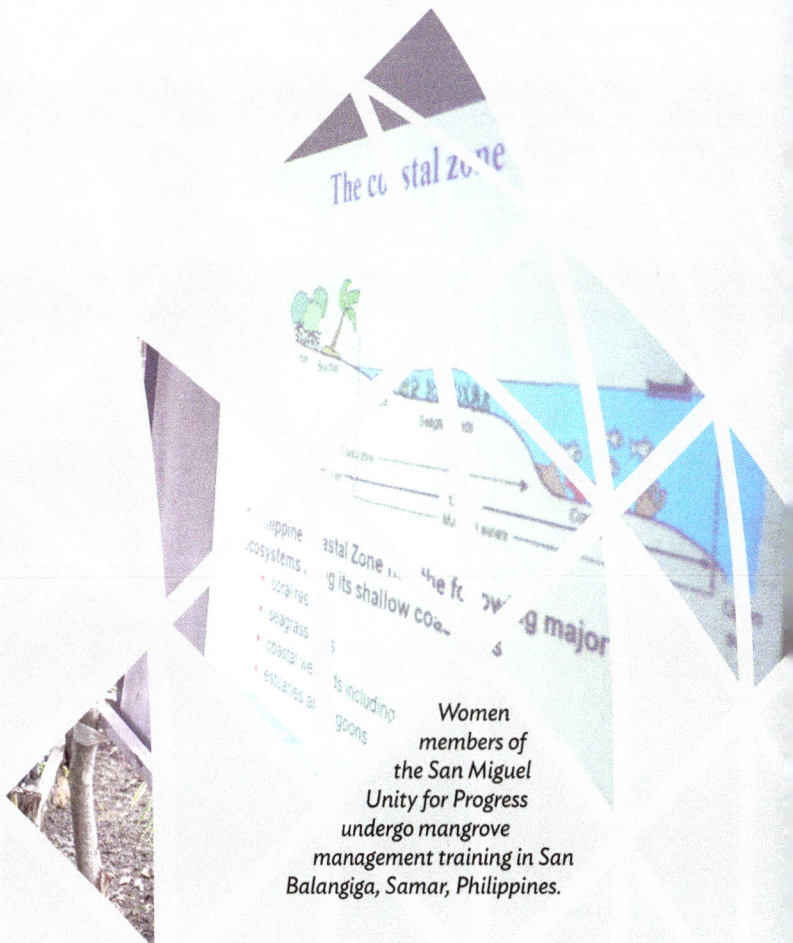

Women members of the San Miguel Unity for Progress undergo mangrove management training in San Balangiga, Samar, Philippines.

This section introduces five characteristics that women-focused investments in climate and disaster resilience should possess (Figure 2). These characteristics were informed by a review of the literature on the nexus of climate and disaster risk, poverty, and gender equality, and also by discussions with stakeholders.

Figure 2. Characteristics of Women-Focused Investments in Climate and Disaster Resilience

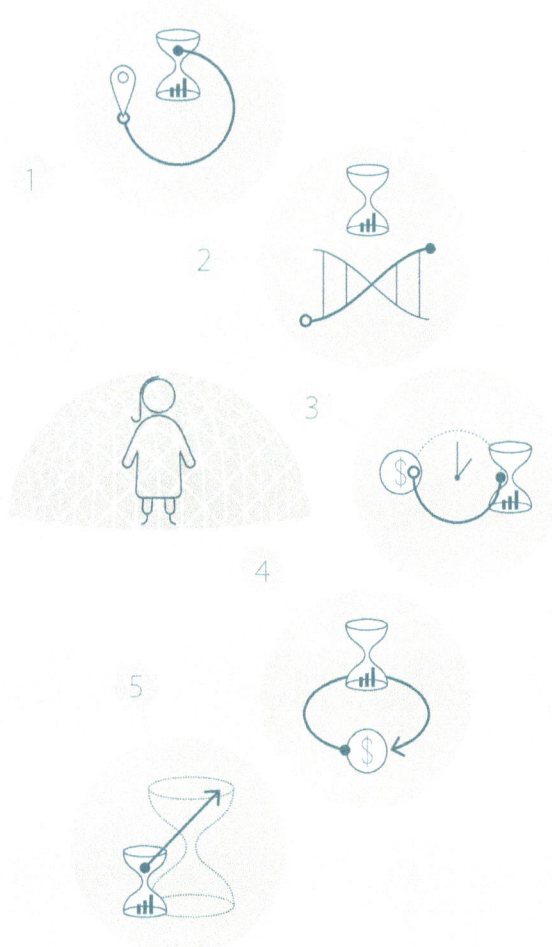

1. Investments Having Women as the Starting Point Based on Robust Understanding of Risks
2. Investments Must Address Structural Inequalities between Men and Women That Lead to the Persistence of Women's Chronic Vulnerabilities
3. Investments that Reduce Women's Time Poverty and Burden of Care
4. Investments That Generate Financial Returns
5. Transformational Investments

Source: ADB.

4.1 Characteristic 1: Investments Having Women as the Starting Point Based on Robust Understanding of Risks

Robust understanding of current and future risk should be the starting point when designing resilient investments. Since risk is a factor of hazard, exposure, and vulnerability, identifying the root causes of risk affecting the sector is important. It is also important to capture the perspectives of both women and men. Evidence shows that women have a deeper understanding of vulnerability, largely due to the role they play in households and the wider community. Because vulnerability links closely to livelihoods and well-being, tapping that knowledge is critical to identifying the most suitable intervention to address risk. Thus, involving women in designing investment projects for resilience becomes crucial.

Resilient-building solutions require a holistic approach to deal with different aspects of resilience, including

- physical (e.g., improved infrastructure);
- ecosystem (e.g., protecting coastal resources);
- social (e.g., diversification of livelihoods); and
- financial (e.g., increased access to crop insurance).

Because the exact nature of an investment project will vary by sector, it will be critical to understand if involving women in the implementation of such investment can help project delivery. Such understanding should also consider the wider benefits the project may gain from involving women in its implementation. For example, when implementing resilience measures, women bundle solutions to manage multiple vulnerabilities in the near and longer term. Examples also show that interventions led by women offer them space for learning, thinking, testing, and adapting to changing conditions (Huairou Commission 2015). As a result, such projects have a greater chance of producing sustainable outcomes. For example, UN Women determined that women's leadership in water management links to more cost-effective water delivery, more households with access to water, and less corruption in water financing (Ray 2016). Thus, while the investment project may support only specific aspects of resilience, the women who participate in implementation may be able to advance other aspects through their informal networks and access to other development programs.

Operation and maintenance (O&M) are critical aspects for achieving resilience, especially with changing patterns of climate hazards. Interventions that address the physical aspects of resilience must consider practical strategies for O&M. Women play a critical role in the successful maintenance of infrastructure assets. Thus, the project design should establish a clear relationship between O&M; the changing nature of climate and disaster risk, where appropriate; and women's potential role in maintenance work.

However, investments should also address the social differences, roles, expectations, and needs of women and men and their different social identities (e.g., status, ethnicity, class, age, religion, and disability between people within these gender categories) (Le Masson 2016; Chaplin et al. 2019).

4.2   Characteristic 2: Investments Must Address Structural Inequalities between Men and Women That Lead to the Persistence of Women's Chronic Vulnerabilities

Structural gender inequalities are major drivers of climate and disaster vulnerability (Ikeda 1995; Neumayer and Plümper 2007; Pearse and Connell 2016; Oxfam 2015), and resilience investments do not automatically challenge them. There is a direct inverse relationship between gender inequality and climate and disaster resilience (i.e., investments in resilience require deliberate consideration of social equity). For instance, when men migrate, women are more likely to choose which crops to plant and have control over land rights and irrigation practices. However, when men return, gender norms often revert, showing the need for interventions that do not challenge the gains that women achieved in the absence of men (GGCA 2016).

Thus, it is critical that women-focused investments to strengthen resilience consciously include interventions to address structural inequalities between men and women, which ultimately will reduce vulnerabilities to climate and disaster risk. Depending on the sector in which the investment project will be implemented, opportunities for addressing such structural inequalities will differ.

In many cases, such interventions will be related to

- policy reforms (e.g., revising the land tenure system);
- revising regulations (e.g., the need to provide collateral for accessing housing microfinance);
- information management (e.g., ensuring that women have access to climate information); and
- capacity building.

Accordingly, investment projects can integrate suitable outputs in the form of capacity building and information management to narrow the gap in structural inequality. In some cases (e.g., investment projects in a post-disaster recovery context where the government is committed to the principles of building back better), there may be opportunities to include outcome indicators to address such structural inequality through changes in policy and regulations.

Implementing such interventions as part of wider sector investment project would benefit from close collaboration with national agencies on women and development. Such collaboration will help identify issues related to structural inequality between men and women in the geographical area in the country, data and information to build evidence, and other initiatives that address similar issues and lessons learned from such initiatives. Discussions with civil society organizations and development partners active in the field of gender and development would be also useful.

4.3   Characteristic 3: Investments That Reduce Women's Time Poverty and Burden of Care

Women-focused investments in resilience should ease women's care burdens in ways that reduce and redistribute labor and time commitments to benefit them directly. Investments in labor-saving assets (e.g., running water, electricity) that allow women to take advantage of new income-earning opportunities are likely to promote better results for their overall well-being and for CCA and DRM strategies. For example, women-led self-help groups in Kenya organized themselves to adopt alternative sources of energy (i.e., biogas), reducing firewood collection time and freeing more time for income-generating activities and participation in the public life of their communities (Huairou Commission 2015).

Similar to other characteristics, the opportunities and scope to address such issues through investment projects will depend on the nature of the sector and the type of investment being envisaged. Many of the interventions in this case may require physical (structural) solutions such as providing child day rooms in agro-processing units, which largely employ women and which can be included as part of project outputs. However, not all structural measures will be directly related to the sector in which the investment project is being designed. Thus, there is need to strengthen collaboration with development programs in other sectors that could support such intervention. For example, infrastructure sectors such as water supply and sanitation, water resources management, and energy can provide concrete opportunities to strengthen resilience and address time poverty. Social sectors (e.g., health, education, social protection) provide ample opportunities to enhance resilience and address burden of care.

4.4 Characteristic 4: Investments That Generate Financial Returns

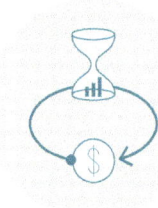

When appropriate, women-focused investments need to generate financial returns. This is especially the case if investments seek the involvement of the private sector. Yet, not every resilient investment, or every component of a resilient investment package, can generate direct financial returns. For instance, an investment that builds physical infrastructure for water conservation to strengthen women's resilience to droughts may have components aimed at increasing women's participation and leadership and changing gender norms about fetching clean water within the household. While the costs of these components are easily quantified (i.e., the budget allocated for implementation), their financial benefits are not easily quantifiable, even as methodological solutions and mechanisms to pay for them increase (Wocan 2013; Homan 2016). Even without generating direct financial returns, projects or components may still generate economic and social benefits (e.g., improved well-being and health of women, women's empowerment). Thus, a different definition of bankability should be adopted depending on the funder (i.e., public, private, multilateral development institutions) and which sector (e.g., energy, housing, industry, and commerce) will deliver the resilience investment; each have a different perspective on bankability (Ellis and Pillay 2017).

4.5 Characteristic 5: Transformational Investments

Women-focused investments in climate and disaster resilience should aim for transformational change by adopting design features that make it more likely. The literature on transformative climate investments has consistently identified four dimensions—relevance, systemic change, scale, and sustainability—that increase the chances of interventions or activities to activate transformational processes and achieve transformational outcomes (Westphal and Thwaites 2016; World Bank Independent Evaluation Group 2016; Global Environment Facility Independent Evaluation Office 2017; ICAT 2018; Puri 2018; Bird et al. 2019; Itad et al. 2019). All four dimensions need to occur — to a greater or lesser extent. Table 2 suggests an interpretation of each dimension in relation to a gender transformative understanding of women-focused investments in climate and disaster resilience. Importantly, transformation is highly sector- and context-specific, so processes, timescales, and outcomes—and what this means for each dimension—will look different in each sector (World Bank Independent Evaluation Group 2016; Global Environment Facility Independent Evaluation Office 2017; Bird et al. 2019; Itad et al. 2019).

Table 2. Dimensions of Transformative Women-Focused Investments in Climate and Disaster Resilience

Dimensions of Transformation	Examples
Strategic relevance refers to the strategic focus of the intervention (i.e., improving women's resilience to the impacts of climate change and natural hazards)	• Investments that are strategically relevant to the national and sector contexts and the objective of increasing women's resilience to climate change and disasters. • Investments that leverage the national and sectoral contexts to increase women's resilience to climate change and disasters (e.g., engaging support from key national champions, aligning with broader initiatives likely to support change processes, integrating political economy considerations).
Systemic change refers to fundamental shifts in structures and functions of the system affecting the resilience of women	• Investments that shift structures and functions in systems and sectors related to women's resilience to climate change and disasters. This includes addressing structural gender inequalities within those systems and sectors.
Scale refers to contextually large-scale transformation processes and impacts in relation to women's resilience	• Investments that seek to increase the climate and disaster resilience of many women, either directly or indirectly, within the national context. This could be achieved through a large-sized investment by design, or the investment itself could be small but have larger impact. • Investments that seek to increase resilience processes and impacts on women and exceed direct investment outcomes (e.g., the replication of mechanisms and models in other resilience investments [scaling up], or uptake from other sectors [scaling out]).
Sustainability refers to the robustness and resilience of changes in relation to women's resilience.	• Processes that strengthen women's resilience activated by the investments are likely to be sustained beyond the investment itself, e.g., uptake of new social norms and behavior enhancing women's resilience, continuity of investments over a longer period of time. • Processes that strengthen women's resilience activated by investments are more likely to withstand new and emerging physical, social, and political shocks and stresses (robustness). • Investments that address social and gender norms to ensure the above two points are delivered and so that changes in resilience are sustained.

Source: Authors' own, based on Bird et al. (2019) and Itad et al. (2019).

5 | IDEAS FOR WOMEN-FOCUSED RESILIENCE INVESTMENTS

This section presents ideas for women-focused resilience investment for agriculture in Cambodia and urban development in Indonesia. Both sectors were chosen for their economic importance. We assessed their transformational potential based on the four characteristics of transformational change—relevance, systemic change, scale, and sustainability—and their importance for strengthening gender equality as well as climate and disaster resilience.

The investment ideas presented here are based on stakeholder interviews in both countries. They are not meant as a comprehensive list of all potential investments. Although the section describes the country context to highlight the importance of these investment examples, resource limitations did not allow a comprehensive review of feasibility (i.e., the political economy). A more in-depth country and sector-specific study would be required to recommend a comprehensive list of women-focused sector investments to build climate and disaster resilience specific to the given socioeconomic, political, cultural, and environmental context and the policy environment within which such investments are designed and implemented.

5.1   Agriculture in Cambodia

In Cambodia, agriculture accounts for around one third of the national GDP. Estimates suggest that 53% of women are employed in the agriculture sector, and activities are predominantly rainfed and subsistence in nature (ADB 2015).

5.1.1   Idea 1: Agricultural Extension Services Targeted toward, Tailored to, and Led by Women

Agricultural producers increasingly need advice and extension services to understand changes in agricultural patterns triggered by climate change and variability, and the risks and potential opportunities that these changes entail (Wiggins and Barrett 2016). By disseminating climate-related information and technologies and supporting climate-sensitive production practices, agricultural extension services contribute to achieving climate-smart agriculture (CSA) (Sala et al. 2016). However, existing delivery of extension services tends to disadvantage women in Cambodia. Generally, extension services agents approach only male farmers because they perceive that women do not farm or that men will share the information with the women in the household (FAO 2011). Information is often delivered primarily through written material, which is inadequate for women because many are less educated, limiting their understanding of the information (FAO 2011). Moreover, while global evidence suggests that women are more likely to adopt climate adaptation strategies communicated by female extension officers (GGCA 2016), that is not happening at scale in Cambodia (Global Forum for Rural Advisory Services 2019). This is problematic because evidence suggests that women are just as efficient as men, and would achieve the same yields when they have equal access to productive resources and extension services (FAO 2011). Thus, it is necessary to find ways to reach women farmers.

CSA extension services reach women when delivered by innovative approaches, including radio, mobile phones, and videos, which allow women to receive information through unwritten material or plant clinics (i.e., face-to-face exchange of knowledge and information between extension workers and farmers), delivered by female agents (Sala et al. 2016). Participatory video approaches featuring local women who improved agricultural practices or share testimonials, and participatory experiential learning providing female farmers with a low-risk setting to experiment with new agricultural management practices, discuss, and learn from their observations, have also been effective (Russo et al. 2016; Sala et al. 2016).

Donors and nongovernment organizations (NGOs) provide most extension services for smallholder farmers in Cambodia. A small number of government extension agents work primarily at the provincial level, and a small percentage are assigned to district Offices of Agriculture, which have no annual budget to deliver services. Female extension agents accounted for only 12% of total staff in 2011. Thus, the government, in partnership with donors, plays a crucial role in expanding the number of female extension agents and delivering women-oriented extension services (Global Forum for Rural Advisory Services 2019).

Transformational change. According to the Ministry of Agriculture, Forestry and Fisheries (2016), women in Cambodia receive only 10% of agricultural extensions services despite comprising 51% of the primary workforce in subsistence agriculture and 57% of the workforce in market-oriented agriculture. Thus, it is highly strategic to invest in women-oriented agricultural extension services, especially because this aligns well with the government's overall ambition to deliver extension services to 5 million farmers by 2020 (Russo et al. 2016).

Evidence suggests that activities run solely by and for women can increase women's willingness to voice their opinions (FAO 2011). If extension approaches are designed to consider women's views and priorities, be flexible with their time preferences and mobility constraints, and ensure their full engagement in disseminating information and adopting new technologies, these features can address structural gender inequalities over time. Moreover, previous research suggests that the introduction of female agents has positive spillover effects for male agents, who become motivated by female agents to increase outreach (Kondylis et al. 2016).

To be sustainable over time, female-oriented extension services need secure land tenure, which rural women identify as a major barrier to economic empowerment (ADB 2015). Taking this factor into account can have a positive and sustainable impact on women's life options and overall well-being, and also on the amount of agricultural production available to support food security and income.

Gender equality. Unequal access to agricultural extension services compounds gender inequality in livelihood opportunities (Kabeer 2015). Evidence from Kenya, Senegal, and Tanzania shows that women with access to extension services can strengthen their position in the household and the community by deciding (jointly with men) how to prioritize planting without having to accept that the man's field will be planted first (Russo et al. 2016). Moreover, more female

extension agents can strengthen women's participation, voice, and agency (Williams 2011), as more of them are able to share their needs and concerns and even attend meetings in the absence of men.

Resilience. The role of agricultural extension and rural advisory services is crucial for supporting CSA, which "sustainably increases agricultural productivity and incomes, and adapt and build resilience to climate change, and reduce and/or remove greenhouse gases emissions, where possible" (Sala et al. 2016, p. 6). Bryan et al. (2018) report that women are more likely than men to use the information they receive, especially regarding

- droughts,
- seasonal weather forecasts,
- information on livestock production,
- forecasts on the start of the rainy season,
- long-term weather forecasts, and
- information on crop production.

Thus, agriculture extension that targets women can lead to significant yield increases in women-cultivated crops (e.g., cassava and vegetables) (FAO 2011), potentially increasing their adaptive capacity and resilience.

5.1.2 Idea 2: Climate-Smart Vegetable Farming through Home Gardens

Almost annually, Cambodia experiences a cycle of floods, especially in the central plains, and drought, likely exacerbated by poorly controlled development and deforestation (Joint Action Group 2015). Most of the rural population rely on subsistence agriculture, and rice by far is the predominant crop. Climate change will also affect food availability, mainly due to the anticipated increase in fish diseases that threaten aquaculture in Cambodia. To cope with the negative effects of climate change, the diversification of agriculture is essential. Investments in climate-smart vegetable farming is a promising option that can allow women already responsible for vegetable production to grow other more profitable crops in different seasons.

Cambodian women in agricultural areas are usually responsible for vegetable production and the sale of surpluses. Such crops include (i) maize, (ii) cassava, (iii) sweet potato, (iv) groundnut, (v) soybean, (vi) sesame, (vii) sugarcane, (viii) tobacco, (ix) jute, and (x) rubber. Women-focused investments in climate-smart vegetable farming (i.e., farming that sustainably increases vegetable productivity and incomes, adapts and builds resilience to climate change, and reduces and/or removes greenhouse gases emissions, where possible) (Sala et al. 2016) can promote women's participation in local markets and, in turn, create opportunities to earn more money and widen their social networks. This is also useful in terms of women's access to information, including early warning for hazards. A key area of gendered climate adaptation that allows women to acts as agents of agrobiodiversity conservation and household resilience involves vegetable gardens or small household plots (GGCA 2016). The adaptation literature suggests that women and men cope differently with climate change. While men usually migrate, home gardens and small-scale agriculture have been a successful strategy for women (GGCA 2016; Aguilar-Støen et al. 2009). Global evidence suggests that women have a unique role in maintaining crop diversity by saving and exchanging seeds and maintaining home gardens (GGCA 2016). Women can use home gardens to reduce expenditure on food items and create their own income by selling their products.

Transformational change. When farm incomes decline and male migration is a major source of income, the relevance of home garden projects remains because women who stay behind and depend on agriculture can benefit from techniques that help them increase food production, raise income, and improve nutrition. Climate-smart vegetable farming is increasingly important because rising temperatures, reduced availability of irrigation water, flooding, and salinity are major factors that challenge vegetable production in Cambodia. (Abewoy 2017). Moreover, food diversity remains a problem, and home gardens that use a climate-smart vegetable farming model show positive results in nutrition indicators and food security (Keats et al. 2017). Finally, the vegetables cultivated in home gardens are usually perceived as having better quality (Keats et al. 2017). Replacing the demand for food imports from neighboring countries with products grown at home and with the potential to be sold within the community is an environmental improvement.

However, investments in climate-smart vegetable farming will need the participation and cooperation of government, multilateral development banks, the private sector, and NGOs to create systematic change. This is demonstrated by the implementation of successful home garden interventions in Cambodia. Keats et al. (2017) show that home gardeners benefit from technical assistance (e.g., how to grow or raise new varieties using ecological practices year-round, sessions on existing crops, training in other new crops) as well physical inputs. These investments, which included training in water, sanitation and hygiene, child feeding, and nutrition, were funded by large-scale public and private donors and implemented by government, local partners, and NGOs. The combination of all these components yielded better results in terms of producing more varieties of vegetables over more seasons, increased food security and dietary diversity, income improvement, and increased sanitary and child feeding practices (Aguilar-Støen et al. 2009; Keats et al. 2017). It is also important that donor investments target high-quality seeds and propagative material. Evidence from Cambodia and elsewhere suggests that this practice can increase not only the quantity of products, but also their variety (Aguilar Stoen et al. 2009; Huairou Commission 2015; Keats et al. 2017).

Smallholder farmers generate more income through increased agriculture product in Thbong Khmum, Cambodia.

In addition, training and introduction of CSA measures (e.g., drip irrigation or biomass briquette production) can also help women improve vegetable production.

In terms of scale, investment models in vegetable farming can be guided in different directions, depending on women's assets, capabilities, and desires. Home garden programs do not need large areas, and the experience of previous interventions suggests that women home gardeners can benefit from public or private investments in subsidized high-quality seeds and propagative materials, tools (e.g., buckets, hoes), earthworms, and even free drinking water filters. Technical and refresher training on agricultural techniques is also important. Likewise, anticipatory investments can pay off. For example, a small irrigation system (e.g., a drip irrigation kit) may protect a home garden against drought. All of these investments can be funded by the government and multilateral development banks, and implemented by the government and local partners. Another option is scaling to high-value supply chains, which would imply a larger and more formal scale of production with more purchased equipment. This would require investments and coordination by public and private donors. To enhance vegetable production, these investments would need increased irrigation. Development of new reservoirs and irrigation canals will be essential and will need coordination between the private and public sectors. However, evidence that the benefits of high-value vegetable supply chains reduce women's vulnerability is mixed. Although not linked specifically to gender outcomes, evidence from Madagascar shows that high-value vegetable contract farming leads to improved productivity of food rice production through technology spillovers, contributing to food availability in the household and shortening periods of food scarcity (Minten et al. 2009). In contrast, the growth of high-value vegetable supply chains was detrimental for women in Kenya because the land and resources they used to cultivate vegetables for home consumption and sale in local markets was appropriated by men for vegetable production under contract (Dolan 2001). Thus, investment in modern value chains should be sensitive to the ways they may support women's livelihoods and challenge gender norms that affect women's positions in their communities and households. When accompanied by technical training specifically aimed at and tailored to women, vegetable farming creates leadership opportunities because women can disseminate knowledge in their communities and become identified as agents of change.

In terms of sustainability, Keats et al. (2017) observe that very few home gardeners dropped out of the program. Indeed, most intended to continue beyond the intervention period because they gained the knowledge they needed and were keen to produce more vegetables with fewer chemicals. Other studies report similar interventions, where women who received vegetable gardens and seed nurseries and learned about related techniques (e.g., post-harvest management and storage) that have shown positive results in different contexts (UNDP 2016, in Uganda; Wiggins and Ghimire 2018, in Nepal). After acquiring knowledge on CSA techniques, women increased their participation as leaders and trainers (UNDP 2016). Thus, getting know-how and leadership skills about vegetable farming and home gardening can help create women's human capital and promote their role as community leaders. These interventions also contribute to more diverse diets and a higher intake of micronutrients (Wiggins and Ghimire 2018). Moreover, women can save money on homegrown food or contribute to household income when they sell their products. Increasing women's income contributes to their long-term economic empowerment and helps build their capacity to cope with environmental shocks and stresses. Overall, evidence shows that vegetable farming is sustainable in the long term, and could be replicated in Cambodia.

Gender equality. Worldwide, women already contribute significantly to their households' food and income through subsistence farming (FAO 2011). However, their contribution is usually invisible or not valued. Investments in climate-smart vegetable farming through home gardens or on their land need to strengthen women's existing activities by removing economic and social barriers that constrain their gains (e.g., land tenure, access to credit, fair price in markets, etc.). Results from a National Adaptation Programme of Action project in Cambodia show that when this happens, men tend to perceive women as contributors to the entire income of the household and support them by fetching water for the vegetables plots (Aguilar et al. 2015).

The experience of home gardens in Cambodia also suggests that although women already participate in vegetable production, their inclusion in home garden interventions is a big positive change compared to previous agricultural extension projects, where women were expected to receive the benefits and information through their husbands, who participated in the training (Keats et al. 2017). However, although gender norms in Cambodia consider women as mothers and bosses, investments in vegetable farming require gender training for men and women to ensure that men do not co-opt the additional income. This way, women are more likely to increase their decision-making power and directly benefit from any additional income. In addition, investments in home garden interventions can use that platform to train women on child feeding, hygiene, sanitation, and food marketing. Based on women's higher attendance at trainings, they show more interest than men (Keats et al. 2017). Training sessions can be provided by the government and NGOs, and the private sector can transmit messages through different channels (e.g., the media or information and communication technology).

Resilience. Innovations in climate-smart vegetable farming promise to improve soil fertility (Wiggins and Ghimire 2018). Likewise, the per unit water footprint of producing certain vegetables and fruits could be relatively low compared to cereals and oil crops. Thus, vegetable production potentially can increase the amount of high-quality food and impose lower environmental burden. Overall, planting a diversity of crops (including intra- and interspecies varieties) associates with resilience to climate change-related hazards (GGCA 2016). Previous research shows that home gardens retain high levels of biodiversity that are maintained and enriched by farming practices, especially plant and seed exchange (Aguilar-Støen et al. 2009). Better results in resilience occur when investments in home gardening are promoted by plant exchange, seed storage, and the dispersion of seeds and plants in different land uses, allowing farmers to encourage plant diversity and consequently increase the resilience of their farming system (Aguilar-Støen et al. 2009).

The Family Farm for the Future project, which offers vegetable seedlings and training on CSA techniques, shows that women's production and income increase, as does their adaptive capacity to cope with climate change and overcome food insecurity (Keats et al. 2017). The project reports that women were able to produce a higher variety of vegetables over more seasons using organic compost and intercropping for insect-pest-management; and improve availability and access to nutritional foods and dietary diversity.

Moreover, smart vegetable production projects implemented by ADB and the Cambodian Rural Development Team showed positive results, decreasing women's vegetable production costs and identifying women as local leaders who can share their knowledge with other community members.

5.2 Urban Sector in Indonesia

In Indonesia, most of the economic growth occurs in urban areas; over 44% of Indonesia's nonpetroleum GDP was produced in cities in 2010 (World Bank 2016). In 2001–2011, 18 out of 21 million new jobs were created in the urban areas (World Bank 2016). Half of the population (118 million) lives in cities, and this is expected to increase to 183 million by 2025 (ADB 2016b).

5.2.1 Idea 1: Women-Operated Decentralized Water Treatment Schemes for Livelihood Diversification

Only around half of the Indonesian population has access to water sources, and around half of the urban population can access safe drinking water. Therefore, decentralized water treatment schemes can offer a solution to water access problems (Hoque 2015; World Bank 2016). In Indonesia, such projects provide a basic model for women-operated decentralized water treatment schemes, whereby women-focused investing can create a value chain that encompasses producing, servicing, marketing, distributing, and selling clean drinking water in urban communities. In local communities, women's groups would form a social enterprise and invest in water purification technologies (e.g., polyethylene filters and an ultraviolet lamp) to collect and treat water sources (e.g., groundwater, rivers and lakes, springs, rainwater).

Water kiosks close to women's homes could be established to house, sell, and distribute the purification systems and bottling systems. Once the clean water is in bottles and containers, women could sell it directly at the kiosk or deliver it to the customer's house for convenience. Women who receive training in marketing, public speaking, and customer service can market the service to new customers. Profit would be reinvested in scaling up the business, or reinvested in other productive enterprises in the community.

Transformational change. Many urban villages and communities lack access to piped water. For example, only 57% of Jakarta's population has piped water (Rosalina et al. 2017). Women already spend a large portion of their time on water-related activities. Therefore, investing in women-operated, decentralized water treatment schemes is a strategic entry point for women-focused investments in climate and disaster resilience. Investments could be within the frame of the Climate Village Program (Proklim), a government-supported but locally owned program to promote CCA at the community level, including water conservation and access to clean water. Many community women's groups, such as the Female Headed Household Empowerment Program, operate Proklims. Overall, there is a strong sense of local ownership in the program.

By fostering a value chain and income-generating employment, the scheme would seek to be financially sustainable. Financial sustainability would allow activities to "professionalize" and empower women through knowledge, skills, and confidence acquisition. This approach has the potential to change established gender norms and power relations that are harmful to women. However, this would not happen organically. Deliberate investment design mechanisms will need to ensure that the changes go beyond the period of the investment itself and that the time women save by getting access to reliable and affordable clean water will help their entrepreneurial skills within the value chain fostered by the scheme, not toward domestic chores.

Gender equality. Safe drinking water is a fundamental and basic need for women's reproductive and productive capacities. Women and girls are usually the primary providers and managers of clean water in the household (ADB and UN Women 2018). They fetch water, often from distant sources, and rearrange household expenditures to buy canister water from suppliers. This can require considerable time. Lack of clean water contributes to disease (e.g., diarrhea). Because women usually care for the sick, children, and the elderly, they are more exposed to infectious diseases. Women-operated, decentralized water treatment schemes would provide a reliable and affordable supply of water, freeing women's time for education, employment, childcare, and rest.

A retail and distribution model centered on women's groups has advantages in terms of (i) providing a pool of women to identify sales agents, and (ii) using women's social networks (i.e., family, friends, neighbors) for marketing and sales. Combined with specific training, these can empower women by developing their entrepreneurial and leadership skills.

Resilience. Being the primary manager of water supply affects women who are adapting to the impacts of climate variability and change, such as seawater intrusion from sea-level rise and flooding and groundwater contamination due to untreated sewage discharges (Pratiwi et al. 2016; Rosalina et al. 2017; Borghardt 2018). Women often cope with such situations by buying canister water, often from expensive vendors. Investing in women-operated, decentralized water treatment schemes would increase their income, help diversify their livelihoods, save their productive and reproductive time, and improve their (and their families') health, therefore, increasing their adaptive capacity.

5.2.2. Idea 2: Bundled Microinsurance for Women to Mitigate Impacts of Natural Hazards in Urban Areas

Indonesia is highly prone to natural hazards such as floods, tropical cyclones, droughts, and earthquakes. Insurance is an important tool for people to manage the residual risks of such disasters. However, women in urban areas currently have very limited access to insurance products. AXA et al. (2015) reported that only 8%–12% of total insurance policyholders in Jakarta are women. This situation results largely from unaffordable insurance services for poorer women. The report also shows that bundled life and health packages are available for around $25 per month (i.e., 5% of women's average salaries). This is high compared to other countries; in the United States, the same package would cost 2% for a woman who earns of $40,000 per year. Microinsurance schemes can help poorer women access insurance services because they are designed to cover those left out of the conventional insurance system (i.e., customers who earn $2–$8 per day); such coverage costs $5–$6 per person per month.

In exchange for a monthly premium payment, microinsurance products address multiple risks, including death of the insured, death of the insured's partner, hospitalization for insured or family members, and loss of livelihood-related assets or home contents. Coverage could be parametric (i.e., payouts triggered when a predefined index threshold is crossed). Microinsurance can protect women against natural hazard-related disasters and allow fast recovery when they happen.

Despite increasing market interests for microinsurance, resulting from products that generally are distinguished by high volumes, low cost, and efficient administration (Insurance Information Institute 2019), multiple barriers still exist for women who seek to purchase insurance to mitigate the impacts of natural hazards in Indonesia, including

- low understanding of how insurance can mitigate the risks associated with natural hazard-related disasters, despite high awareness of the frequency of natural hazards in the country;

- lack of targeted products for urban women. The most popular products are credit-life policies, which pay a policyholder's debt when they die, and agricultural index insurances; and
- hard-to-reach and geographically fragmented customers, due to Indonesia's many islands (AXA et al. 2015).

There is scope for the government to implement a microinsurance scheme that offers innovative women-targeted bundled products in partnership with private insurance and microfinance companies to mitigate the risks of natural hazards. Multilateral development partners can support the government design and launch the scheme and by providing financing as needed. Private insurance and microfinance institutions can operate as contractors and payers of services, enrolling beneficiaries, and settling claims. They would train female agents and brokers and also implement awareness campaigns and marketing initiatives to acquire female clients (Wiedmaier-Pfister and Miles 2016). In addition, the government could facilitate the creation of innovative distribution models for insurance products (e.g., mobile channels) by ensuring that the underlying policy and regulatory environment, as well as infrastructure systems, support the models. The current infrastructure for information technology in Indonesia does not fully support such an offering (AXA et al. 2015).

Transformational change. Considering the high frequency of natural hazards in Indonesia, disaster microinsurance products have great potential due to

- the experience of the microlending industry in South and Southeast Asia, which shows that women likely will be better and more profitable clients than men. This has led to the creation and increasing success of microinsurance schemes and products for women (Wiedmaier-Pfister and Miles 2016);
- the predicted high growth of the insurance sector. Estimates suggest that women will spend $9–$14 billion on premiums by 2030, approximately 10–16 times higher than 2013 ($0.9 billion) (AXA et al. 2015); and

- the strong incentive of insurance companies to work with stakeholders to ensure that microinsurance schemes for women serve as "transition products" to conventional insurance services as their income increases over time. Women's income doubled in 2010–2015 (AXA et al. 2015).

Microfinance companies have a strong incentive to employ women as brokers and agents in their distribution channels because client service managers are better at reaching female clients. Early evidence shows a correlation between the percentage of women in the salesforce and the percentage of women retail clients in Asia (AXA et al. 2015). As the industry continues to grow, women's greater involvement will contribute to their empowerment through increased income and status, potentially challenging existing gender norms.

Gender equality. Bundled microinsurance products targeting women are successful because they address women's dual roles as workers and caretakers of the family. For instance, in India, a women's insurance cooperative created by VimoSEWA developed a product that pays women members a certain amount per day, not only for their own hospitalization, but also for family members. This feature recognizes that women may lose pay if they have to spend time in the hospital caring for a family member (Wiedmaier-Pfister and Miles 2016). Thus, companies should structure their products to mitigate the risks of women's "double burden" in the event of a shock to their own and their family members' lives.

Resilience. Women often rely on negative recovery strategies after a disaster (e.g., taking high interest loans, selling important assets, or drawing on important savings (Patel and Bhatt 2016). According to World Bank estimates, 18% of Indonesian women carry outstanding loans for health and emergencies (Wiedmaier-Pfister and Miles 2016, p.3). Microinsurance coverage would greatly improve women's absorptive capacity, especially if the product covers livelihood activities (e.g., trading of goods such as urban garden vegetables, fish products, etc.). Microinsurance would also contribute to the resilience of the wider community because urban local goods are important in a post-disaster recovery (Patel and Bhatt 2016).

6 | ENABLING ENVIRONMENT REQUIRED TO DELIVER WOMEN-FOCUSED INVESTMENTS IN RESILIENCE

Rubysol transports back to the barangay the crab traps she and her father laid the other day in the mangrove forest just outside their barangay in Pilar, Surigao del Norte, Philippines. Her family is a beneficiary of the conditional cash transfer program (4Ps) of the Government of the Philippines.

A supportive and "enabling environment" is critical to delivering women-focused investments in climate and disaster resilience. This includes an ensemble of the policies, laws, capacity, institutions, governance, incentives, evidence, and data.

6.1 Policy, Regulation, Planning, and Implementation

Efforts to strengthen women-focused investments in climate and disaster resilience requires support from policy makers (GGCA 2016). Further, recognizing the key leadership role of women in national climate change and DRM policy is crucial to translating women's needs, priorities, and perspectives into concrete investments. Ideally, policy makers should share a long-term vision of what such investments look like. This shared vision will guide the formulation, implementation, and evaluation of long- and medium-term national plans.

However, the mere existence of policy and regulatory frameworks is not enough. For instance, a country may have well-developed gender and climate change policy frameworks, but often they are not well implemented in the day-to-day operation of line ministries. Thus, strengthening climate and disaster resilience should be an explicit priority of sector plans and investments, and their linkage with the role women could play in driving adaptation should be established. For example, a country can emphasize adaptation in agriculture and water resources, where women are largely employed and present.

Within the planning process, budgeting is a fundamental enabler of achieving women-focused resilience investments. Requirements for a certain percentage of the budget could be earmarked for women-focused investments across all projects. Legal requirements, operational guidelines, and capacity building for gender-responsive resilience planning and budgeting should be in place at all line ministries and subnational governments. These steps can have a big influence in countries undergoing a strong decentralization processes.

Whenever possible, monitoring, evaluation, and learning systems and processes should adopt adaptive principles (i.e., the objective of women-focused resilience investments do not change, but the pathways to achieving them must respond to the changing context (USAID 2018). This will require implementation arrangements, indicators, annual

work plans, and budgets. Capacity should be built throughout all levels to ensure that those working at the nexus of climate change, disasters, women's empowerment, and wider socioeconomic development have the necessary knowledge and skills to deliver women-focused investments in climate and disaster resilience.

Planning a clear articulation of the project pipeline is fundamental to delivering women-focused investments that involve the private sector. Without signaling needs clearly, private investors cannot commit to spending on the measures necessary for investment (e.g., due diligence, credit-evaluation). The private sector already finances many investments in adaptation and mitigation efforts such as innovative clean energy and climate-related technologies. However, procedures should be developed to ensure that women's concerns and priorities are integrated into policies, interventions, and incentive mechanisms for private sector investments (Williams 2011).

6.2 Evidence and Data

Although planning for women-focused resilience investments should build on large-scale quantitative studies, which could improve the ability to generalize findings, and also on qualitative gender-sensitive studies that provide insights on location-specific analyses of climate and disaster vulnerability, such studies are lacking in many cases. Even when focusing on quantitative indicators (e.g., health, education, employment, and assets), conventional gender analyses are challenged by the collection and analysis of data, especially at the subnational level. For instance, a country's socioeconomic assessments may sort data by male- and female-headed households. However, we need to step forward with an integrated sex- and, ideally, age-disaggregated data system among all ministries that support program formulation.

6.3 Horizontal and Vertical Coordination and Capacity Building

Women-focused investments need improved coordination and communication at all levels of government and also at the project level. For instance, provincial and city governments may suffer gaps due to different levels of commitment to adapting to climate change. This will require greater vertical integration among municipal, provincial, and national governments on policies and practices that aim to build women's resilience to climate change and disasters.

Similarly, horizontal lesson-sharing and coordination around women-focused investments across sectors and between different ministries and subnational offices would help support locally appropriate solutions and accelerate action on best practice. These could be in the form of technical working groups or task groups, which could be embedded within projects through project steering committees.

More work is needed to build the capacity of ministries and sector agencies, which traditionally do not work at the nexus of gender equality, poverty alleviation, climate change, and natural hazards, to understand the importance of promoting women-focused investments in climate and disaster resilience, and how this can be achieved. Importantly, some governments may want to frame this issue differently, using language such as "equality between women and men," "gender equality," or "women's empowerment." Thus, capacity building should be framed around the language that is used by national governments and key stakeholders in a way that it pursues clear actions.

6.4   Inclusive and Risk-Informed Governance

Women-focused investments should provide opportunities for women to engage in dialogue with national and local governments and ensure consideration of women's practical needs, interests, vulnerabilities, and capacities in policy, plans, and standards. This will require strengthening the institutions and processes that provide the necessary space to support and deliver such an approach (e.g., decentralization programs that enable women's involvement in bottom–up planning and budgeting processes). In terms of participation in decision-making, training, or other activities, evidence suggests that meetings with only women or with an equal number of men and women can increase women's willingness to voice their opinion (FAO 2011). This aspect is important when thinking about women-focused investments to strengthen climate and disaster resilience.

Additionally, supporting resilient development initiatives led by grassroots women's organizations is an important starting point that can motivate local governments to support bringing investments to scale, ensuring successful outreach to vulnerable women and identifying their practical needs. For instance, global evidence shows that geographical expansion and institutional adoption of programs by governments, donors, and NGOs increase successful grassroots strategies led by women for building community resilience via (i) organic and sustainable agriculture, (ii) water sources revival, and (iii) alternative energy projects (Huairou Commission 2015).

From a development perspective, investments must be informed by risk. Only a gendered understanding of current and emerging climate and disaster risk can ensure that interventions will not create or increase existing vulnerabilities or exposure to natural hazards.

A lack of "bankable" projects—understood here from a private sector perspective as projects deemed unlikely to deliver high enough risk-adjusted returns to attract private equity or debt—is major issue for climate investments in mitigation and adaptation. Governments should play a crucial role in mitigating such risks, including enabling (i) environmental risks, (ii) the willingness of project consumers or end-users to pay risks, (iii) technology risks, and (iv)macroeconomics risks (i.e., credit, liquidity, exchange rate, interest rate, and economic growth) (Nassiry et al. 2016).

7 | CONCLUSIONS

A family overlooks several hectares of cabbage patch. As with others in the region, irrigation and a second-hand tractor have increased yields dramatically in Pak Xong village, Lao People's Democratic Republic.

This report argues for the need, opportunity, and scope of strengthening women-focused investments in climate and disaster resilience. It provides conceptual clarity on which issues these investments should address and what they should feature. Investments should seek to strengthen women's existing capacities to anticipate, absorb, and adapt to the impacts of natural hazards and climate change and contribute to the achievement of the 2030 Agenda for Sustainable Development. Moreover, investments should have women as the starting point of investments, be financially sound, and seek transformational change.

Investments in women's resilience to natural hazards and climate change should consider the following core principles:

- Investments must address structural inequalities between men and women that lead to the persistence of women's chronic vulnerabilities.
- Investments should recognize and promote women's existing capacities and build their resilience by strengthening their capacity to adapt to, anticipate, and absorb the impacts of natural hazards, including those influenced by climate change and variability.
- Investments must benefit women, not just co-benefits or unwanted burdens.
- Investments should be designed and implemented by women, who should be the primary beneficiaries and/or users.
- Investments should seek to generate financial returns where possible.
- Investments should seek to create transformational change.

Women-focused investments in climate and disaster resilience require coordination and planning among ministries and national agencies of planning and finance, women and development, sector development, DRM, and CCA. This report presents a few practical examples of how women-focused investments can increase climate and disaster resilience through sector efforts in agricultural development in Cambodia and urban development in Indonesia. Providing a more in-depth, country- and sector-specific list of women-focused investments to build climate and disaster resilience will require additional studies, specific to the given socioeconomic, cultural, and environmental context and policy environment for which these investments are designed and implemented.

Finally, this report indicates several enabling factors that could help different ministries make progress in delivering women-focused investments in climate and disaster resilience. Such factors include (i) an ensemble of good policies, regulations, and investment plans; (ii) solid implementation; (iii) available and high-quality evidence and data for programming; (iv) horizontal and vertical coordination among ministries, different levels of government, and development partners; and (v) risk-informed and inclusive governance that leverage existing women's groups and institutions and provide processes for women's participation. Where appropriate, these factors lead to inform decision-making and the implementation of plans and programs.

References

Abewoy, D. 2017. Review on Impacts of Climate Change on Vegetable Production and Its Management Practices. *Advances in Crop Science and Technology. 6 (1). pp. 330.*

Asian Development Bank (ADB). 2013. *The Rise of Natural Disasters in Asia and the Pacific: Learning from ADB's Experience.* Manila.

_____. 2015. *Promoting Women's Economic Empowerment in Cambodia.* Manila.

_____. 2016a. *Achieving Universal Electricity Access in Indonesia.* Manila.

_____. 2016b. *Indonesia: Country Partnership Strategy (2016–2019).* Manila.

_____. 2018. *Strategy 2030: Achieving a Prosperous, Inclusive, Resilient, and Sustainable Asia and the Pacific.* Manila.

ADB and Huairou Commission. 2017. *Accelerating Sustainable Development: Investing in Community-Led Strategies for Climate and Disaster Resilience.* Manila: ADB and Huairou Commission.

ADB and UN Women. 2018. *Gender Equality and the Sustainable Development Goals in Asia and the Pacific. Baseline and Pathways for Transformative Change by 2030.* Bangkok: ADB and UN Women.

Aguilar-Støen, M., S. Moe, and R. Camargo-Ricalde. 2009. Home Gardens Sustain Crop Diversity and Improve Farm Resilience in Candelaria Loxicha, Oaxaca, Mexico. *Human Ecology.* 37(1). pp. 55–77.

Aguilar, L., M. Granat, and C. Owren. 2015. *Roots for the Future: The Landscape and Way Forward on Gender and Climate Change.* Washington, DC: International Union for Conservation of Nature (IUCN) and Global Gender and Climate Alliance (GGCA).

Anon. 2018. INDOPOS. indopos.co.id. https://indopos. co.id/read/2018/10/24/153487/33- lokasi-raih-penghargaan-program-kampung-iklim-tahun-2018 (accessed 22 February 2019).

Allen, M.R. et al. 2018. Framing and Context. In Masson-Delmotte, V. et al., eds. *Global Warming of 1.5°C. An IPCC Special Report on the Impacts of Global Warming of 1.5°C above Pre-industrial Levels and Related Global Greenhouse Gas Emission Pathways, in the Context of Strengthening the Global Response to the Threat of Climate Change, Sustainable Development, and Efforts to Eradicate Poverty.* Geneva: IPCC.

AXA, Accenture, and IFC. 2015. *SHEforSHIELD: Insure Women to Better Protect All.* https://www.ifc.org/wps/wcm/connect/a2d8348049d01b0c82a5a3e54d141794/SheforShield_Final-Web2015.pdf?MOD=AJPERES (accessed 23 February 2019).

Bahadur, A. et al. 2015. *The 3As: Tracking Resilience across BRACED.* London: Overseas Development Institute. https://www.odi.org/publications/9840-3as- tracking-resilience-across-braced.

Belkhir, J. and C. Charlemaine. 2007. Race, Gender and Class Lessons from Hurricane Katrina. *Race, Gender and Class.* 14(1/2). pp. 120–152.

Bielenberg, A. et al. 2016. *Financing Change: How to Mobilize Private-Sector Financing for Sustainable Infrastructure.* New York City: McKinsey Center for Business and Environment.

Bird, N., Y. Cao, and A. Quevedo, A. 2019. *Evidence Synthesis on Transformational Change in the Climate Investment Funds.* London: Overseas Development Institute.

Borghardt, S. 2018. *Gender Analysis of GIZ Project "Integrated Resource Management in Asian Cities: The Urban Nexus"—Indonesia.* Bangkok: UNESCAP.

Bradshaw, S. and M. Fordham. 2013. Women, Girls and Disasters. A Review for DFIF. https://assets. publishing. service.gov.uk/government/uploads/system/uploads/attachment_data/file/236656/women-girls- disasters. pdf.

Bryan, E., Q. Bernier, and C. Ringler. 2018. *A User Guide to the CCAFS Gender and Climate Change Survey Data.* Washington, DC: International Food Policy Research Institute (IFPRI).

CARE International. 2015. *Gender Dynamics in a Changing Climate: How Gender and Adaptive Capacity Affect Resilience. Gender Dynamics in a Changing Climate: Learning from the Adaptation Learning Programme for Africa.* Nairobi: CARE International.

CARE-West Africa. 2015. *The Resilience Champions. When Women Contribute to the Resilience of Communities in the Sahel through Savings and Community-Based Adaptation.* Accra: CARE West Africa. http://careclimatechange.org/publications/%20 resilience- champions/.

Carpenter, S. et al. 2014. From Metaphor to Measurement: Resilience of What to What? *Ecosystems.* 4 (2001). pp. 765–781.

Center for Excellence in Disaster Management and Humanitarian Assistance. 2017. *Cambodia Disaster Management Reference Handbook*. Hawaii: Centre for Excellence in Disaster Management and Humanitarian Assistance.

Chanthy, S. and H. Samchan. 2014. Flood Impacts on Women: Exploring the Possibility of Gender- Sensitive DRR planning. A report submitted to ActionAid Cambodia.

Chaplin, D., J. Twigg, and E. Lovell. 2019. *Intersectional Approaches to Vulnerability Reduction and Resilience Building—A Scoping Study*. Resilience Intel. London: BRACED.

Chopra, D. and C. Muller. 2016. Introduction: Connecting Perspectives on Women's Empowerment. *IDS Bulletin*. 47(1). pp. 1–10.

Diwakar, V. et al. 2019. *Briefing Note - Child Poverty, Disasters and Climate Change: Investigating Relationships and Implications over the Life Course of Children*. London: ODI and CPAN.

Diwakar, V. and A. Shepherd. 2018. Sustaining Escapes from Poverty. *ODI Working Paper*. London: Overseas Development Institute.

Dolan, C.S. 2001. The 'Good Wife': Struggles over Resources in the Kenyan Horticultural Sector. *Journal of Development Studies*. 37(3). pp. 39–10.

Dougherty, S. et al. 2016. Climate Change Vulnerability Assessments in Indonesia: Where are the Women's Perspectives? *Asian Cities Climate Resilience Working Paper Series*. No. 37. London: International Institute for Environment and Development.

Ellis, C. and K. Pillay. 2017. Understanding 'Bankability' and Unlocking Climate Finance for Climate Compatible Development. *CDKN Working Paper*. London: Climate and Development Knowledge Network. https://southsouthnorth.org/wp-content/uploads/2018/09/Working-Paper_Unlocking-Climate-Finance.pdf.

Engle, N.L. 2011. Adaptive Capacity and its Assessment. *Global Environmental Change*. 212: pp. 647–656.

Ergas, C. and R. York. 2012. Women's Status and Carbon Dioxide Emissions: A Quantitative Cross- National Analysis. *Social Science Research*. 41(4). pp. 965–976.

Food and Agriculture Organization of the United Nations (FAO). 2011. *Women in Agriculture, Closing the Gender Gap for Development. The State of Food and Agriculture, 2010–2011*. Rome.

_____. 2013. Cambodian Farmer Harvests Fields of Gold. *MALIS Newsletter*. 1 (January). http://www.fao.org/3/a- at645e.pdf.

Folke, C. 2006. Resilience: The Emergence of a Perspective for Social–Ecological Systems Analyses. *Global Environmental Change*. 163. pp. 253–267.

Fordham, M. and S. Gupta. 2011. *Leading Resilient Development. Grassroots Women's Priorities, Practices and Innovations*. New York: United Nations Development Programme and GROOTS International. http://www.undp.org/content/dam/aplaws/publication/en/publications/womens-empowerment/leading-resilient- development—grassroots-women-priorities-practices- and-innovations/f2_GROOTS_Web.pdf.

Gass, P., H. Hove, and J.E. Parry. 2011. Review of Current and Planned Adaptation Action: East and Southeast Asia. PreventionWeb.net. [online].

Global Gender and Climate Alliance (GGCA). 2016. *Gender and Climate Change: A Closer Look at Existing Evidence*. Washington, DC.

Global Environment Facility (GEF), Independent Evaluation Office. 2017. *Review of GEF Support for Transformational Change*. Paper prepared for the GEF 52nd Council Meeting. USA. 22 May 2017. https://www.thegef.org/council-meeting-documents/review-gef-support- transformational-change.

Global Forum for Rural Advisory Services. 2019. *A Brief History of Public Extension Policies, Resources and Advisory Activities in Cambodia*. http://g-fras.org/en/ggp-notes/94-world-wide-extension-study/asia/south-eastern-asia/287-cambodia.html#top.

Guilbert, K. 2017. In Drought-Hit Niger, Women's Savings Could Be Route to Resilience. *Building Resilience and Adaptation to Climate Extremes and Disasters*. 5 November. http://www.braced.org/news/i/?id=efb15d0e-da35- 4b1a-aa11-0abbe1195ffc.

Holling, C.S. 1973. *Resilience and Stability of Ecological Systems. Annual Review of Ecology and Systematics*. Vancouver: University of British Columbia.

Holmes, R. and N. Jones. 2013. Key Concepts in Gender and Social Protection. In *Gender and Social Protection in the Developing World: Beyond Mothers and Safety Nets*. London: Zed Books.

Homan, R. 2016. *Costing of Social Norm Interventions—A Primer for the Passages Project*. Washington, DC: Institute for Reproductive Health, Georgetown University.

Hoque, U. 2015. Summary of Indonesia's Gender Analysis. *ADB Papers on Indonesia*. No.6. Manila: ADB.

Huairou Commission. 2015. *Community Resilience at Scale: Grassroots Women Demonstrating Successful Practices.* http://www.wocan.org/ resources/ community-resilience-scale-grassroots-women-demonstrating-successful-practices#.

Ikeda, K. 1995. Gender Differences in Human Loss and Vulnerability in Natural Disasters: A Case Study from Bangladesh. *Indian Journal of Gender Studies.* 2(2). pp. 171–193.

Initiative for Climate Action Transparency (ICAT). 2018. *Transformational Change Guidance—Guidance for Assessing the Transformational Impacts of Policies and Actions.* Copenhagen: UNEP DTU Partnership and World Resources Institute.

International Food Policy Research Institute. n.d. *Agricultural Extension.* http:// www.ifpri.org/topic/ agricultural-extension.

International Institute for Sustainable Development (IISD). 2011. *Review of Current and Planned Adaptation Action: Southeast Asia.* Winnipeg.

Intergovernmental Panel on Climate Change. 2012. *Managing the Risks of Extreme Events and Disasters to Advance Climate Change Adaptation.* Geneva.

Insurance Information Institute. 2019. *Background on Microinsurance and Emerging Markets.* https://www.iii.org/article/background-on- microinsurance-and-emerging-markets#Insurance%20In%20Emerging%20Markets,%202017.

Itad, Ross Strategic, and ICF International. 2019. *Evaluation of Transformational Change in the Climate Investment Funds.* London: Itad.

Joint Action Group. 2015. *Joint Action Group Positions: Disaster Risk Reduction in Cambodia.* Phnom Penh. https://www.humanitarianresponse.info/sites/www.humanitarianresponse.info/files/documents/files/khm_0801_drrpos_alljagpositions_en_0.pdf.

Kabeer, N. 2015. Gender, Poverty, and Inequality: A Brief History of Feminist Contributions in the Field of International Development. *Gender and Development.* 23 (2). pp. 189–205.

Keats, S., S. Sokcheng, and P. Dary. 2017. *Scaling Up Home Gardens for Food and Nutrition Security in Cambodia.* Phnom Penh: Overseas Development Institute and Cambodia Development Resource Institute.

Khan, N. 2016. Sexual and Gender-Based Violence in Natural Disasters: Emerging Norms. *Commonwealth Law Bulletin.* 42 (3). pp. 460–468.

Kondylis, F. et al. 2016. Do Female Instructors Reduce Gender Bias in Diffusion of Sustainable Land Management Techniques? Experimental Evidence from Mozambique. *World Development.* vol. 78 (February). pp. 436–449.

Lavell, A. et al. 2012. Climate Change: New Dimensions in Disaster Risk, Exposure, Vulnerability, and Resilience. In Field et al., eds. *A Special Report of Working Groups I and II of the Intergovernmental Panel on Climate Change (IPCC).* Cambridge and New York: Cambridge University Press.

Le Masson, V. 2016. *Gender and Resilience from Theory to Practice: Working Paper.* BRACED Programme. London: Overseas Development Institute.

Le Masson, V. et al. 2016. *Disasters and Violence Against Women and Girls. Can Disasters Shake Social Norms and Power Relations?* London: Overseas Development Institute.

Marcus, R. 2018. *The Norms Factor. Recent Research on Gender, Social Norms and Women's Economic Empowerment.* London: International Development Research Centre and Overseas Development Institute.

McKinsey Global Institute. 2015. *The Power of Parity: How Advancing Women's Equality Can Add $12 Trillion to Global Growth.* New York: McKinsey and Company.

Meerow, S., J.P. Newell, and M. Stults. 2016. Defining Urban Resilience: A Review. *Landscape and Urban Planning.* 147: pp. 38–49.

Ministry of Agriculture, Forestry and Fisheries. 2016. Climate Change Priorities Action Plan for Agriculture, Forestry and Fisheries Sector, 2016–2020. Technical Working Group for Policy and Strategy to Respond to Climate Change of the Ministry of Agriculture, Forestry and Fisheries (TWG-CCAFF). Phnom Penh.

Ministry of Environment, Royal Government of Cambodia. 2006. *National Adaptation Programme of Action to Climate Change (NAPA).* Phnom Penh.

Minten, B., L. Randrianarison, and J. Swinnen. 2009. Global Retail Chains and Poor Farmers: Evidence from Madagascar. *World Development.* 37 (11). pp. 1728–1741.

Nassiry, D., S. Nakhooda, and S. Barnard. 2016. *Finding the Pipeline: Project Preparation for Sustainable Infrastructure.* London: Overseas Development Institute.

Neumayer, E. and T. Plümper. 2007. The Gendered Nature of Natural Disasters: The Impact of Catastrophic Events on the Gender Gap in Life Expectancy, 1981–2002. *Annals of the Association of American Geographers.* 97 (3). pp. 551–566.

Nugent, C. and J.M. Shandra. 2009. State Environmental Protection Efforts, Women's Status, and World Polity: A Cross-National Analysis. *Organization and Environment*. 22 (2). pp. 208–229.

Onarheim, K., J. Iversen, and D. Bloom. 2016. Economic Benefits of Investing in Women's Health: A Systematic Review. *PLoS ONE*. 11 (3): E0150120.

Opitz-Stapleton, S. et al. 2019. *Risk-Informed Development: From Crisis to Resilience*. New York: Overseas Development Institute and United Nations Development Programme.

Oxfam International. 2015. The Tsunami's Impact on Women. *Oxfam Briefing Note*. Nairobi. https://oxfamilibrary.openrepository.com/bitstream/handle/10546/115038/bn-tsunami-impact-on-women-250305-en.pdf;jsessionid=C9A37AF7470E03D8258810DF5E48C922?sequence=1.

Patel, R. and M. Bhatt. 2016. Innovating and Testing Small Business Disaster Microinsurance for Urban Resilience. *Humanitarian Exchange*. No. 66 (April). pp. 35–37. https://odihpn.org/wp-content/uploads/2016/04/HE-66-Web-Final.pdf.

Pearse, R. and R. Connell. 2016. Gender Norms and the Economy: Insights from Social Research. *Feminist Economics*. 22 (1). pp. 30–53.

Pratiwi, N.A.H., Y.D. Rahmawati, and I. Setiono. 2016. Mainstreaming Gender in Climate Change Adaptation. *Asian Cities Climate Resilience Working Paper Series*. No. 39. London: International Institute for Environment and Development.

Puri, J. 2018. Transformational Change—The Challenge of a Brave New World. *Independent Evaluation Unit, Learning Paper*. No. 1. Songdo: Green Climate Fund. https://ieu.greenclimate.fund/documents/315504/318369/Working_Paper_Transformational_Change_-_The_Challenge_of_a_Brave_New_World.pdf/96702562-0e1d-3e9a-a9cc-bbea65103bbe.

Ray, I. 2016. Investing in Gender-Equal Sustainable Development. *Discussion Paper: World Survey on the Role of Women in Development*. New York: UN Women.

Republic of Indonesia. 2017. *Indonesia: Third National Communication Under the United Nations Framework Convention on Climate Change*. Jakarta.

Ringler, C. et al. 2017. *Climate Change, Gender and Nutrition Linkages. Research Priorities in Cambodia. Feed the Future*. Washinton, DC: Feed the Future: The U.S. Government's Global Hunger and Food Security Initiative.

Robinson, J. 2015. *Gender Sensitivity in Disaster Management*. Berlin: Oxfam and DanChurchAid. https://www.humanitarianresponse.info/en/operations/cambodia/document/gender-sensitivity-disaster-management.

Rosalina, E. et al. 2017. *Gender into Urban Climate Change Initiatives (GUCCI) in Indonesia—Status Quo Report on Jakarta and Makassar*. Berlin: GUCCI in Indonesia.

Russo, S., C. McOmber, and E.P. McKune. 2016. GACSA CIS and Gender Analysis. In S. Sala, F. Rossi, and S. David, eds. 2016. Supporting Agricultural Extension towards Climate-Smart Agriculture: An Overview of Existing Tools. *COMPENDIUM: Climate-Smart Agriculture and Extension*. Rome: Global Alliance for Climate-Smart Agriculture, FAO.

Sala, S., F. Rossi, and S. David, eds. 2016. Supporting Agricultural Extension towards Climate-Smart Agriculture. An Overview of Existing Tools. *COMPENDIUM Climate-Smart Agriculture and Extension*. Rome: Global Alliance for Climate-Smart Agriculture, FAO.

Sidner, S. 2011. Solar Panels Power Profit in Bangladesh. *CNN Going Green*. 12 April. http://edition.cnn.com/2011/BUSINESS/04/11/bangladesh.solar.power.kalihati/index.html.

Tatlonghari, G. 2014. Gendered Adaptations to Climate Change: The Case of Rice Farming Communities in the Philippines. A thesis submitted for the degree of Doctor of Philosophy. Monash University, Australia.

Udry, C. et al. 1995. Gender Differentials in Farm Productivity: Implications for Household Efficiency and Agricultural Policy. *Food Policy*. 20 (5). pp. 407–423.

United Nations Development Programme (UNDP). 2007. *Energy and Poverty in Cambodia. Challenges and the Way Forward*. Regional Energy Programme for Poverty Reduction, UNDP Regional Centre in Bangkok. New York: UNDP.

_____. 2016a. *Gender, Climate Change Adaptation and Disaster Risk Reduction. Training Module 2*. New York.

_____. 2016b. *Gender and Climate Change. Gender, Climate Change and Food Security*. New York.

United Nations Environment Programme (UNEP). 2016. *Adaptation Finance Gap Report, 2016*. Copenhagen: UNEP DTU Partnership (UDP). http://www.unepdtu.org/newsbase/2016/05/uneps-adaptation-finance-gap-report-released?id=377aa3d4-32c1-4100-8bee-ae65390b60ba.

United Nations. 2018. *The Sustainable Development Goals Report, 2018*. New York. https://unstats.un.org/ sdgs/files/report/2018/ TheSustainableDevelopmentGo alsReport2018-EN.pdf.

UN Women. 2017. *Understanding Cost-Effectiveness of Gender-Aware Climate Change Adaptation Intervention in Bangladesh*. New York. http://asiapacific. unwomen.org/en/digital-library/ publications/2017/09/ understanding-cost-effectiveness- of-gender-aware- climate-change.

———. 2018. Why Gender Equality Matters for All the SDGs. In UN Women. 2018. *Turning Promises Into Action: Gender Equality in the 2030 Agenda for Sustainable Development*. New York. https://www. un-ilibrary.org/women-and-gender-issues/turning- promises-into-action_917ed83e-en.

United States Agency for International Development (USAID). 2018. *Discussion Note: Adaptive Management*. https://usaidlearninglab.org/library/ discussion-note-adaptive-management.

Wiggins, S. and S. Barrett. 2016. Towards a Coherent and Cross-Sectoral Policy Framework for Food Security and Nutrition. *Guidance Note on Climate Change*. London: International Institute for Environment and Development and Overseas Development Institute.

Wiggins, S. and A. Ghimire. 2018. *Country Report: Innovations for Terrace Farmers in Nepal and Testing of Private Sector Scaling Up Using Sustainable Agriculture Kits and Stall-Based Franchises*. Ottawa: International Development Research Centre.

Williams, M. 2011. *Ensuring Gender Equity in Climate Change Financing*. New York: UNDP.

Westphal, M. and J. Thwaites. 2016. *Transformational Climate Finance: An Exploration of Low-Carbon Energy*. Washington, DC: World Resources Institute.

Wiedmaier-Pfister, M. and K. Miles. 2016. *Mainstreaming Gender and Targeting Women in Inclusive Insurance: Perspectives and Emerging Lessons. A Compendium of Technical Notes and Case Studies*. Bonn: GIZ. http:// www. munichre-foundation.org/dms/MRS/Documents/ Microinsurance/2016_IMC/Presentations/PS11- IMC2016-Presentation-Green/PS11%20IMC2016%20 Presentation%20Green.pdf.

Women Organizing for Change in Agriculture and Natural Resource Management. 2019. *About the W+ Standard. W+ Standard: Ensuring Benefits to Women*. http://www.wplus.org/about-wplus.

Woetzel, J. et al. 2018. *The Power of Parity: Advancing Women's Equality in Asia Pacific*. New York: McKinsey & Company.

World Bank Independent Evaluation Group. 2016. *Supporting Transformational Change for Poverty Reduction and Shared Prosperity*. Washington, DC: World Bank IEG. https://ieg.worldbankgroup. org/ evaluations/supporting-transformational-change- poverty-reduction-and-shared-prosperity.